# WHAT'S NOT TO LOVE?

## Poetry by
## Rose McConahy

Published by Purple Unicorn Media



ISBN 978-1-910718-10-0

Cover photograph *Crows At Dawn* by Elizabeth Frerichs

*Rehabilitation For The Soul* previously published in Innovate Magazine January 2015

# DEDICATION

This collection of poetry dedicated to my sister, Monique Renee Hogue and her daughter, Casondra Conrad. In loving memory of Monique's son, Joshua Craig Strosnider, who left this world too soon. His journey, a lesson to live life to its fullest and his heart, taught us all. Josh became the wind which caresses our cheeks and to dry our tears. His rebel soul touched many, and in all my years I had never seen such an outpouring of love. Ride the wind Bud, and carry our love with you. We will see you again.

# ACKNOWLEDGEMENTS

Special thanks to Robert P. Broadwater, for without your generous heart and expertise, I would never have pursued my passion.  Thank you to Altoona Writer's Guild for encouraging others and your support.  You are a great group of talent.  I would also like to thank my son, Edward McConahy.  Eddy, you believed in me before I believed in myself.  Thank you and I love you forever. Mert, may you find some sort of peace from the words within these pages.  You and your family have given love to so many people; I can only hope to give you some kind of comfort.

## ~CONTENTS~

# INTRODUCTION

Inspiration lurks in most unusual places. Perception is key. Finding our way back from despair is a journey we have all encountered. Signs of inspiration when the darkness is unrelenting, tests our human resolve. However, there are signs. Whether shadowed by grief or simply unfamiliar, we have all traveled this road. When a mother's nightmare enters reality, and unimaginable sorrow present, love still triumphs.

Death points its finger at life, and while raw emotion discouraged, we must continue on for our journey incomplete. Loss of a loved one positions us in the forefront of our souls. We begin to acknowledge truth hidden within and question what is beyond. Perhaps that is why we are forced to experience it...

May you find peace in your darkest hour.

# WHAT'S NOT TO LOVE?

# TEARS OF GRATITUDE

No shame in tears
Cry as you might
Every pearl a whisper
I love you.

Love the goal
Mission of the soul
With depths of eternity
Wondrous world, to behold.

To feel the grandeur
a gift from beyond.
To feel the pain
a price of love.

The Universe gives
but must receive
and every tear
says thank you.

# TO TRULY LIVE

A wild child
from the get go
with a mind made up
and a spirited soul.

Routines and schedules
deemed shackles of life
and try as one might
he'd wiggle away.

No bondage for the soul
conformity kept at bay
for somehow he knew
to live, meant this way.

To exist, insufficient
for life, an adventure
and true to himself
he lived.

# THIS WAY MAMA

I see my lessons
in the forest.
Not among
man made words.

My spirit
guides me,
the beaten path
goes unheard.

I thank you Mama
your gentle hand
but my answers lay
within the wind.

Your heart my beacon
for weathered storms.
Your love my savior
when my soul torn.

Try as I might
cannot conform
for the ways of this world
broken, and unsure.

# YOU MADE OUR HEARTS SING

Strummin' his six string
his path foretold.
The road he followed
a gift bestowed.

Passion at his fingertips
Music from the soul
Shared with this world
Compassion he holds.

His gypsy genes
On he'd go
Embraced the hearts
of all who got to know.

Our ramblin' man
Our breath for life
The musician who brought
song, into our lives.

## PLEASE, OH PLEASE

Tears of greed
we shed for you.
More our need,
time with you.

Please don't leave
our love for you.
The souls grieve
our loss of you.

Homeward bound
our hearts agree
but selfishness
dictates our pleas.

Unanswered prayers
we receive
as spirit rises
and rides free.

Graced by your touch
Dropped to our knees
Our hearts break
when your soul, leaves.

## WHY?

One of our own
travels past knowledge.
Summoned home
his wings arrived early.

Our world tilted
scales out of balance
and our inner compass
spins out of control.

Unanswered questions
and unanswered prayers
stole the life
given to you.

No parent
should ever endure
good bye to their child,
destination unsure.

# ILLUMINATION OF LOVE

Candles alight
each don a name.
Celebration
of eternal life.

Memories
our chauffeurs sometimes
to carry us
in our darkest times.

A flame
the breath of a soul
touched our lives
then time to move on.

When love burns
and the heart says so,
time nor distance
can extinguish, the light.

# A MOTHER'S LOVE

Sweet child,
Sweet child of mine
Morrow never the same
For your eyes no longer shine.

Blessed once
Blessed twice
Fruit of the womb
Divine.

Introduced to love
Above all other kind
Sweet child,
Sweet child of mine.

# HAND IN HAND

In darkest times
Obvious the light
For even a sliver
A beacon in the night

It is then:
We find comfort
It is then:
The heart begins to realize.

Our grief
A measure
Of love
Divine

Cast out the shadows
which clog the mind.
Embrace the darkness,
the light will shine.

Without one
we cannot find,
the path to lead us
to the other side.

**ETERNAL**

A mother's love
fierce and forever
no matter where
her cub roams.

This realm
or the next
eternity
makes it so.

Hand in hand
love and heartache
for this world
beautiful, yet cold.

But a child
loved by a mother
never
alone.

## REBEL SOUL

Dismiss.
I cannot.
Ignore.
Impossible.

Summons from within
cast out, in these times.
In order to fit
one must realize.

A rebel soul
not one size for all.
Desires outside the box
Expectations, too small.

Live to the fullest
opinions in the wind
for true to thyself
individual, mission.

Accepted by few
more envy than sin
to walk the walk
from the call within.

# OFF THE BEATEN PATH

Into the briers
before one knows
off the trampled path
pain tells you so

The ups and downs
they come and go
life too smooth
isn't living at all.

Risks and rewards
Travel companions
One without the other,
taste of life bland.

Roadside has its worth
forge ahead to discover
for simply to sit
a waste you cannot recover.

Venture on
Create a new path
Explore this world
and never look back.

# UNANSWERED QUESTIONS

Truth lays dormant
Imagination climbs
Speculation takes over
sanity, questions the mind.

Lack of answers
an uphill trek.
The heart creates a version
the mind struggles to accept

Unexpected anything
Blindsides of life
but a knife to the soul
the toughest kind of strife.

Robbed of forever
Stolen time together
The question remains,
Why, Oh why?

# TREASURE THE MOMENT

Dismiss the future.
Weed out the past.
Live in the moment
treasures to be had.

The coin in the sky
or soil beneath your feet,
gems all around
for any who seek.

Petals appear
Trees live and breathe
Earth Mother provides
abundance for needs.

No guarantees
one day to the next
for many not granted
longevity, as a gift.

# TRUE SELF



Your journey in life
always your own
true to yourself
admiration I've known.

Resist to conform
knew not for you
Your soul your leader,
good for you.

Adventures abound
discoveries await
your tune a solo
your heart, sate.

Harder the road
in modern day
but onward you'd go
the old soul knew the way.

Past our lives
you travel now
and pave our way
for meet again, we shall.

## RECOGNIZABLE SOULS

A Cheshire grin
and a twinkle in the eyes.
Your beautiful face
ingrained in my mind.

Gone,
but not gone at all
for your pulse
lives in my soul.

Memories,
the puppeteers of time.
Keep you alive
until side by side.

Dreams,
our bridge for now
for the breath of love
cannot let go.

Souls,
identical tempo,
time nor space
can separate.

# HI BABY

The call of the crow
grabs my attention.
A message
from the other side.

Messengers I'm told
Stories from the wise,
and I listen
to intuition.

Safe your journey
No longer alone,
as you sit on a wire
before my very eyes.

I inquire
and your caw responds
eye to eye
then off you go.

Message received
Free as the wind
Silent the worry
we'll see each again.

**LOVE ETERNAL**

A memory created
by the heart and soul
can never fade
will not let go.

A footprint in time
eternal the flow
for the soul's memory,
flawless.

The perfect gem
in every light,
our facets within
known as insight.

From first to last breath
our memories we store,
those with love involved
allowed through the door.

Here our garden grows
Be selective of seed
for a crop to sustain,
once past, this reality.

# PENNIES FROM HEAVEN

Mourning
turns to numbness
Days pile up
like penny stacks.

Each penny a memory
Gifts from Heaven
Time allotted
with those we love.

Once parted
all which remains
are the pennies
and the love.

# REMINDERS OF LOVE

Loss of kin
awakens the heart.
Memories flood
the forgotten gates.

Levies break
we can only hold on
or swept away
by our sorrow.

Heartbeats echo
and the soul chimes in.
Questions arise
about purpose again.

Days have lacked
Love spread thin
To remind perhaps
live and love now – not then.

# IF ONLY I HAD KNOWN

If I had known
the last hug,
never would I let go.

If I had known
the last words,
I would have told you more.

If I had known
the last encounter,
better my attention.

If I had known
the last spoken I love you
still, I couldn't love you more.

# TAKE WHAT YOU NEED

Here are my wishes
you may have my dreams too,
anything of mine
freely I give to you.

For need or comfort
I'd give it all
to wash away pain
or smother it all.

Talons of the Reaper,
scars upon your chest.
How can I help?
I'll take care of the rest.

Life sent you a curve
bean-balled the soul,
and though devastated,
you are not alone.

Take my hand through this plight
let me guide you for a time.
No mother should endure
an unfair game, in life.

# ONCE YOU MET JOSH



In all my years
sight unseen
an outpour of love
from each you meet.

Shattered hearts
scattered like pick-up sticks,
each in their own time
to be pulled from the rubble.

Never before
the impact of love.
Never before
the bells of sincerity.

In such darkness
light pours forth
for the love you created
once through our door.

Now you've crossed over
a stampede of grief
but all you have given
will lift us from our knees.

# OUR LOVE FOR YOU

Many hearts
weep for you.
Minds consumed
by memories.

Our greed
desires you to stay
but our souls know
you're meant to be on your way.

A journey here complete
a loss insufferable indeed.
We beg the powers that be
offer you your dreams.

Forget not,
the souls of your past.
Forever in our hearts
the love will last.

Grateful to know you
no solace at this point.
May the wind be beneath you
until again, we are joined.

# OUR SOULS WILL ALWAYS RECOGNIZE

We've gazed from mountain tops
and crawled the valley floors
you as my spotter
and I as yours.

A journey from childhood
forced to endure
but as we walk now
stronger than before.

Two souls joined
by others hands.
How grateful am I
together we stand.

Friends for life;
Sisters by heart.
Familiar souls
which will never part.

# THE MEASURE OF LOVE



Life's toughest test
came to your door
forced its way in
rocked your world.

Up-ended order
Knocked you to the floor
But battered and bruised
your love held true.

A mother's weakness,
breath of a babe.
Bound and gagged
watched life slip away.

Bones turn to jello
heart turns to shards
yet still you give
for another's regard.

Strength when you're broken,
love's final test.
Continue to live
as your young man soars.

# NO BOUNDARIES FOR LOVE



Each milestone in life
ignites the memories
when the candle of love
burned bright.

Snuffed by tears
of humans' plight,
but insight
does not cease there.

The boundaries
of the trained mind
limit love,
confine.

But love eternal
Shadows of no kind –
Cannot be,
confined.

Through walls of realms
the power flows,
once in a heart
on and on, it goes.

# MONIQUE

If you need a laugh,
a comedian I become.
If you need to weep,
a shoulder waits for you.

If you want to scream,
I will bellow with you.
If you want silence,
I will sit beside you.

If you cannot see,
my arm to guide you.
If you cannot breathe,
take my air for you.

Whatever you may need,
whatever you desire.
Regardless of reach,
it is yours.

# TAKE MY HAND

Dark the abyss
which calls your name
summons you
from depths of pain.

Unsteady the Mother
teeters on the edge
but before then
a sister to me.

Grab my hand
you cannot go
cannot allow
a sacrificed soul.

Trained a warrior
your weakness spotted
but you're not alone
for your back I hold.

Demons attacked
loss of our own
we will rebuild
yet not, forget the fallen.

# DON'T WALLOW TOO LONG

Death points a finger
at your life and mine.
Rethink priorities
Reevaluate time

Troll the wastelands too long
no further the path
for woes and worries
certain the trap.

Troubles and grief
encounters for all
but stronger and wiser
those who brush them off.

Added weight on our journey
shortens our trek.
Quicksand exists
and hungers, for souls.

# YOUR JOSHUA TREE



A symbol indeed
in more ways than one.
Grown from a seed
nurtured by love.

Not unlike
Casey and I,
your Joshua tree
here to remind.

Warmth from your laughter
and guidance by your hand
allowed me to prosper
into a young man.

My gratitude, these roots
for your love keeps me near
and somehow, someway
the three of us will persevere.

Grow with me Mama,
reach out from the darkness
with every breath, and every branch
we are with you.

# LOVE LIVES ON

Shed the tears
let them flow
for the heart to weep
love lives on.

Memories hold
slideshows of life.
A path created
lit by light.

His hand in yours
you started out,
for guidance needed
with a child.

Each journey our own
you learn to let go
but clear to the soul
you love him so.

He crossed realms,
no hand to hold.
Your heart weeps
and yet, he lives on.

## LIGHT OF LIFE



Light flickers
as winds of sorrow
blow through the cracks
of the shattered heart.

Loss of love
of any kind
gale force beats
against the shutters.

Barriers break
Emotion overflows
Marinates the bones
Saturates the soul

The light of life
tries to weather the storm
but all the unknown
detours galore.

Struggles for a path
One to comprehend
Preserve the light
Begin again

# THE DAY OUR WORLD CHANGED

Dim lights
Faded hues
One second
All it took

A child
Your child
Crosses over
To paradise

Snuffed light
Darkness
Your heart
Consumed

Shrieks
In the night
Tears
And confused

Love endures
In a world
Tainted
By death.

# THE AIR WE BREATHE

A tender heart
raw from heartache
love ripped out
by the hand of fate.

Loss never easy
and bolder the love
deeper,
the scar.

Some never heal
simply layers of tissue
to keep air at bay
and soften the sting.

Crippled inside
we limp through reality
all the while
just try to breathe.

**JOSH RIDES**

Numb -
Confusion and heartache
But the world would pause
if they'd met your son.

A smile that melts butter
Humor from the heart
Compassion his way
right from the start.

Ingrained in his soul,
life meant to be lived.
Ride the iron horses,
born free to the end.

Paved his own way
and gave all along.
Touched hearts of many,
created his own song.

Admiration I carry
Grateful my heart
To claim the title aunt
To love you all along.

Ride with the wind,
Sing to us when you can
Numb and confused
I cannot comprehend.

# YOUR JOURNEY CONTINUES



Search for an Eden
led you away
away from this world
away from modern day.

A free spirit
tracked by restraints.
A feather in the wind
hounds lose the scent.

One step ahead
your motto for life.
True to yourself
your heart your guide.

Unable to mold
a virtue of its own.
Admire the strength
for the road long.

No paradise here
time to move along
as the wings of your soul
carry you home.

# OUR LOVE

Your friends have a void.
Your mother's heart crushed.
Your sister lost
by the sudden hush.

All pray you knew
how much you're loved
as the tear stains
swallow any pride.

Gone from our lives
but never our souls
for your memory carries
our grief to the light.

Your charm and wit
blessed our days.
Your smile,
always so bright.

A beacon for us all
unconditional the love.
May you find peace
in the heavens above.

# MY SISTER

Daily we talk
share, laugh, and cry
no other I know
rather spend time.

One hand a sister
the other a friend.
How blessed to share
this journey to the end.

Finish a sentence
read each minds
through sorrow and joy
past the end of time.

Souls connected
a mate for life
eternity guarantees
we'll always be joined.

Grateful for you
my sister, my friend
Let's give them hell
then do it again.

## STILL...

A gentle breeze
Assurance
Sun filled day
Seeps within

Confirmation
You still exist
Not in the way
The mind trained

Yonder
Then beyond
Our souls extend
Past comprehension

We lag behind
The progression
Of the open mind
And sated heart

Your playground now
On the Milky Way
You're home now
Among the stars

## OUR JOURNEY

Hands held through labor
the journey begun.
A handful from the get go
blessed by your son.

Adventures abound
for the old soul seeks
but a changed world
unkind and bleak.

No matter to the babe
What's here? What's there?
Runs his veins
Octane to his air

True to himself
no restraints at all.
A child of the Universe
loved by all.

We'll hold hands today
simply to stand
for the weight of his journey
too much to bear alone.

A door he's discovered
the threshold he crossed
onward he goes
we absorb the loss.

Grateful our time
lucky to have known
not a goodbye
just a need to roam.

Sisters remain
can't shoulder alone
as the son of one
rides toward the sun.

## ORGAN DONOR

Life given
after your own.
Last selfless act
presence carries on.

A piece of yourself
for another's breath.
Look upon this earth
no regrets.

You taught us love
and take ours with you
as you soar the vastness
better suited for you.

Changed lives,
filled our hearts.
Ride in peace
by the love within you.

# SOULS YOU TOUCHED

Family after family
claim you as their own
for so many hearts
you touched as you roamed.

Selfish not
the bones within you
for the love you spread
grew a garden of Eden.

For it is we
who should of nurtured thee
but the lessons you taught
every soul sees.

Live
wild and free,
truth to thyself
gentle hands toward man.

Many mourn
as your journey continues
but each holds a part
of the heart you shared.

Never goodbye,
See you again,
for the souls
will recognize.

# PARADE OF LOVE

Steel horses roar
rumble in the streets,
honor thy brother
his journey here complete.

Grown men weep
for the hands of Josh
embraced their hearts
unacceptable loss.

Their code a bit different
their brother still rides
on the wings of the wind
always by their side.

Younger than most
but love has no age.
A good man respected,
hearts changed.

Memories will come and go
but Josh will remain,
for  many have loved
and life, never the same.

# MEET YOU AT THE BRIDGE



Loved ones wait
for those left behind.
Other side of bridge
elimination of time.

Tears create rivers,
need for a bridge.
Even the Universe
cannot separate love.

No desire to sever
that which gained
as the soul's purpose
for our existence.

We are made to seek
the heart our guide.
Harder the task
in these here times.

Rest assured
opportunity to cross,
those your heart holds
are never lost.

## SONGS OF JOSH

Each time I hear a chime
I'm reminded of you
for when the wind blows
you whisper a tune.

A soul of the Universe
privileged to know you
but now you ride
and your heart sings.

On tails of comets
through endless skies
born to be free,
gone before your time.

Our love travels with you
and pieces of our hearts.
Please continue to sing
then you're not as far.

With shattered hearts
and souls which weep,
this world didn't hold
what you needed to seek.

# LETTERS TO HEAVEN



Survival of another day
she glides ink across the page.
Pours out her heart
to reach out, to the beyond.

No side by side chatter
the laughter's gone
with pen poised
she shares her life.

Hugs, part of history
but words live on
as does the love of a son
who's moved on.

Letters to Heaven
for the bond still strong,
time not a factor
when two souls belong.

Dear Josh – they begin
Love Mom – their end
as the void in her life
shrinks with the pen.

# AFTER THE LOSS OF LOVE

Through darkened tunnels
then up Mount Everest
the heart's path
to mend.

Never to be whole again
but to live without love
not to live, at all.

We sacrifice pieces
share parts of our souls
all, in the name of love.

Expose our weaknesses
Reveal our desires
For to risk,
the only way.

Til' our death
the burden stays
on the heart
which once loved.

# GRATITUDE OF A SECOND



One second
past the eyelids open.
One second
before reality slams home.

All the sands
trapped in a glass,
one grain
of peace.

Loss of a loved one
bitter the taste
but loss of an only son,
life incomplete.

A moment of ignorance
the only reprieve
as the mind awakes, remembers
the heart and soul's grief.

One second of peace
life's become,
all which is left
to hold on to.

# THIS WORLD COULDN'T HOLD YOU

Once a tot
but always loved.
A young man called
to the heavens above.

Too grand the heart
too wise the soul
to linger this earth
onward must go.

Broken hearts
left on the trail
but true to himself
holds, to no avail.

Graced by his presence
Honored to know
Touched by his life
Luck bestowed.

Ride on
born to be free
with satchels packed
our hearts, you take with thee.

# LOVE GOES HOME



A soul departed
Rivers halt
Time paused
and the heavens, wait.

A concoction
Mixed emotions
Our loss
another's gain.

Pulled asunder
for love peaked,
as we're reminded
of our home.

Your ascent
Taunt strings
Tethered to our creator
and our hearts.

We learn peace
as rivers begin to trickle
and time lends, a gentle hand
to pull us, from our grief.

# ROAD TO ACCEPTANCE

Scar tissue begins
on the shards of the heart.
Shattered from love
when the call came in.

Your wings sprouted early,
called home too soon.
Those who love you
crumbled inside.

Blindsided.
Kicked in the teeth.
A mother's nightmare
enters reality.

But alone
she is not
for hundreds mourn
our loss.

Time offers up
peace of its own
dependent upon
manipulation, of our thoughts.

## FIRST EXPERIENCES WITHOUT YOU

The first of many
this journey without you.
The first birthday
no way to hug you.

The first holiday
only a picture to view.
An empty chair
in honor of you.

The first six months
since you changed realms
instead of adding years
we trudge through hell.

The first of many
life without you
and now we wait
for the first smile.

## DON'T SIT THERE



You see an empty chair
but a loved one rests there.
To rest their wings
which enabled them, to be there.

Their journey
led them away
but our love
allows them to return.

Every milestone
they share,
for love
eternal.

The heart,
the keepsake
through realm
after realm.

Our memories
the highways
maintained
by the souls.

# IN THE WIND



Four months
to this day,
we honored you
and sent you on your way.

The next leg
of your journey,
unprepared hearts
in your wake.

And though we know
you had to go,
our greed
still wants to hold you.

Selfish our tears
for our souls speak
you are where
you need to be.

Ride the wind
which is your soul,
forever remember
you are loved.

## SAMHAIN

The veil thins
whispers
we'll see each again.

From your world
into mine
souls greet,
a pause in time.

The sheerest lace
separates
as hearts yearn
for one another.

Day of the dead
we celebrate,
for love
travels time.

# THANKSGIVING BLESSING

Today we give thanks
from broken down hearts.
Need to reach deep
find our gratitudes.

This year slammed us hard
for the loss of a child.
Loss of any child,
weighs on a weary soul.

But this boy I speak of,
one of our own.
One of our babies
summoned home.

Our world destroyed
Tears overflow
How to go on,
an answer unknown.

Today we give thanks,
I guess to have known.
The smiles, the laughter,
baby's breath grown.

## NO DOUBT ABOUT IT

No doubt lingers
in this soul of mine.
You conquered love
in your short amount of time.

And though your journey
ended too soon,
labeled a success
for our hearts grew.

Stumbled along,
rocky road given you
yet you lifted
the one beside you.

Battered and dusty,
your spirit smiled
and touched another
all the while.

You soar with angels
never a doubt
for your love remains
in the hearts, of your wake.

# GRANTED A LONG LIFE



Brittle bones
Swollen joints
Price of life
Past the prime

Earned the aches,
gifted the time
for not all
as lucky.

Granted the right,
to reminisce
to reflect
and realize.

This realm
a teacher.
This time
a test.

My purpose
hidden.
My life
the quest.

# WHAT'S NOT TO LOVE?

Ebony marbles
reveal your love.
Sheppard's hair
comes and goes.

Beautiful boy
Handsome man
Through it all
his Mama stands.

Just to the side
for room he'd be needin'
the spirit demands
wind for fleein'.

Meant to soar
truth can't be denied
and Mama's breath
catches each time.

I love you she says
to the twinklin' eye
What's not to love Mama?
What's not to love.

# DONATE LIFE

Organ donation saves lives.  Josh's last selfless act was being an organ donor.  Multiple families have their loved ones with them today because of this generous act.  CORE which is the Center of Organ Recovery and Education, worked with our family with the utmost compassion and gratitude.  A team guided us and strived to understand our pain.  Many people are on waiting lists for organs.  Families are on the brink of despair.  Please consider registering to become an organ donor.  For more information, please check out their website at www.core.org

# PURPLE UNICORN MEDIA

www.purpleunicornmedia.com